GREETINGS CARDS

Devised and illustrated by

Clare Beaton

Kingfisher Books

Contents

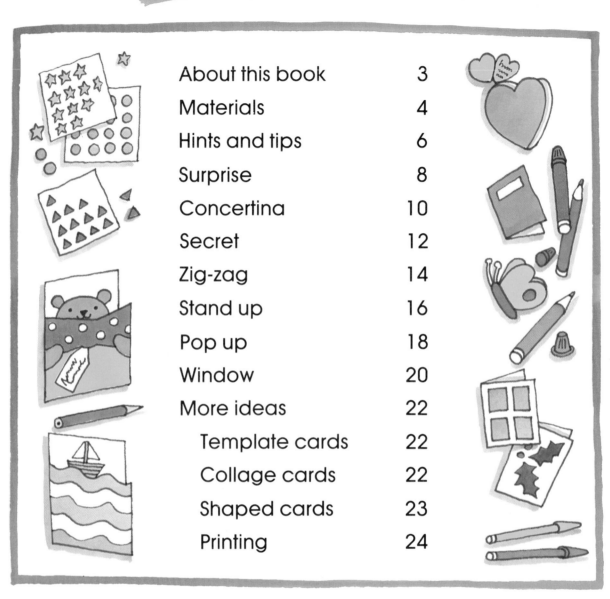

Produced for Kingfisher Books by
Tony Potter, Times Four Publishing Ltd

Conception and editorial:
Catherine Bruzzone, Multi Lingua

Kingfisher Books, Grisewood & Dempsey Ltd Elsley House,
24-30 Great Titchfield St, London W1P 7AD

First published in 1990 by Kingfisher Books

Typeset by TDR Photoset, Dartford
Colour separations by RCS Graphics Ltd
Printed in Spain
British Library Cataloguing in Publication Data
Beaton, Clare
  Greeting cards
  1. Greetings cards. Making – Manuals – For children
  I. Title II. Series
  745.594
ISBN 0 86272 512 7

About this book

This book will show you some easy and fun ways to make greeting cards. There are step-by-step instructions for seven main card designs and ideas for lots more at the end of the book.

On the left-hand pages, there are four simple steps to follow:

On the right-hand pages, there are more ideas for you to try out with the same design.

The simplest cards are at the beginning of the book and the more complicated ones at the end. You should be able to find most of the materials you need in your home. Look at pages 4-7 for some helpful hints.

You can make the easiest cards very quickly but will need to plan, and perhaps shop, for some of the others. At the end of the book you will find ideas for making a lot of cards of the same design, for example for invitations.

Materials

Remember that you will probably want to put your cards in an envelope, so make sure they fit. You might like to buy or make envelopes first, so that you know what size to make the cards. Also, don't use very thin paper or the cards won't stand up. You may also have the same problem if you make them too large. Here are some of the many kinds of paper you can use.

Keep old wrapping paper to use in collages or to cover cards.

Use patterned papers as cut-outs or backgrounds.

Paper with letters or numbers is useful to cut up for names or birthday cards.

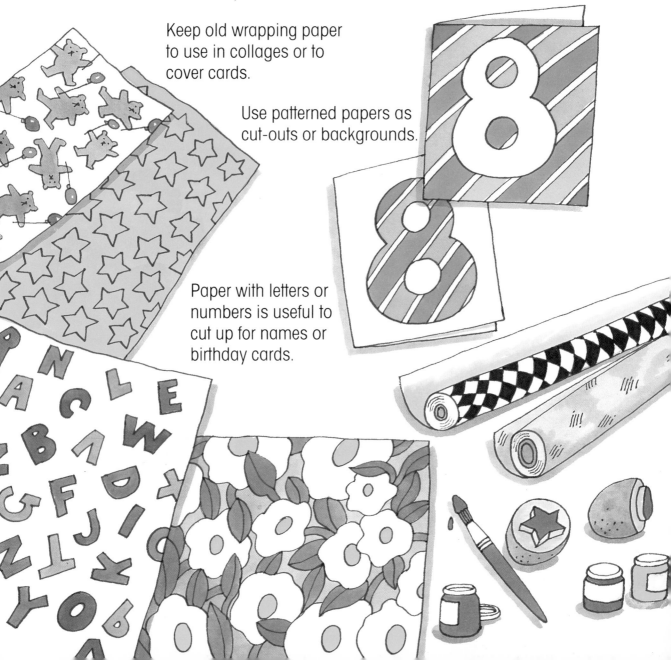

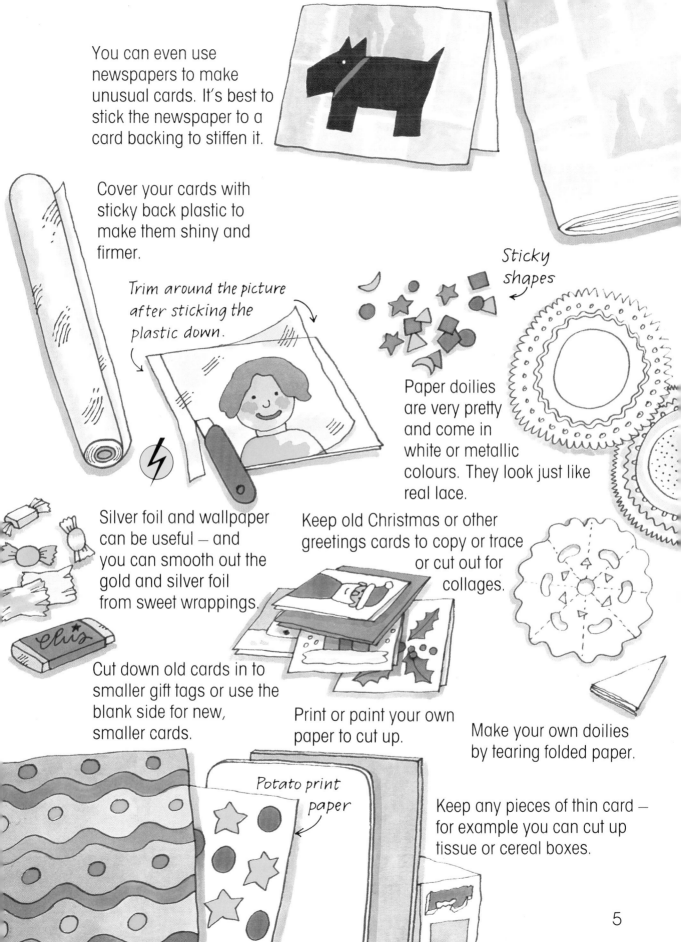

You can even use newspapers to make unusual cards. It's best to stick the newspaper to a card backing to stiffen it.

Cover your cards with sticky back plastic to make them shiny and firmer.

Trim around the picture after sticking the plastic down.

Sticky shapes

Paper doilies are very pretty and come in white or metallic colours. They look just like real lace.

Silver foil and wallpaper can be useful — and you can smooth out the gold and silver foil from sweet wrappings.

Keep old Christmas or other greetings cards to copy or trace or cut out for collages.

Cut down old cards in to smaller gift tags or use the blank side for new, smaller cards.

Print or paint your own paper to cut up.

Make your own doilies by tearing folded paper.

Potato print paper

Keep any pieces of thin card — for example you can cut up tissue or cereal boxes.

5

Hints and tips

Keep drawing things together in a box where you can find them easily. Look after them carefully and they will last a long time and work well. Always keep paper flat. It takes time to flatten a roll of paper out.

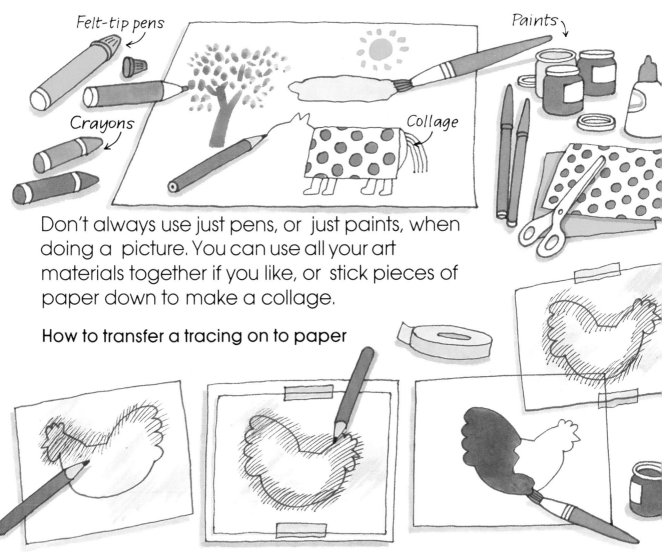

Felt-tip pens

Crayons

Paints

Collage

Don't always use just pens, or just paints, when doing a picture. You can use all your art materials together if you like, or stick pieces of paper down to make a collage.

How to transfer a tracing on to paper

1 Turn the tracing over and pencil all over the back of the picture.

2 Turn it over again and stick it in place on the paper. Draw along the lines in pencil.

3 Take off the tracing paper and go over the line in pen or paint in the shape.

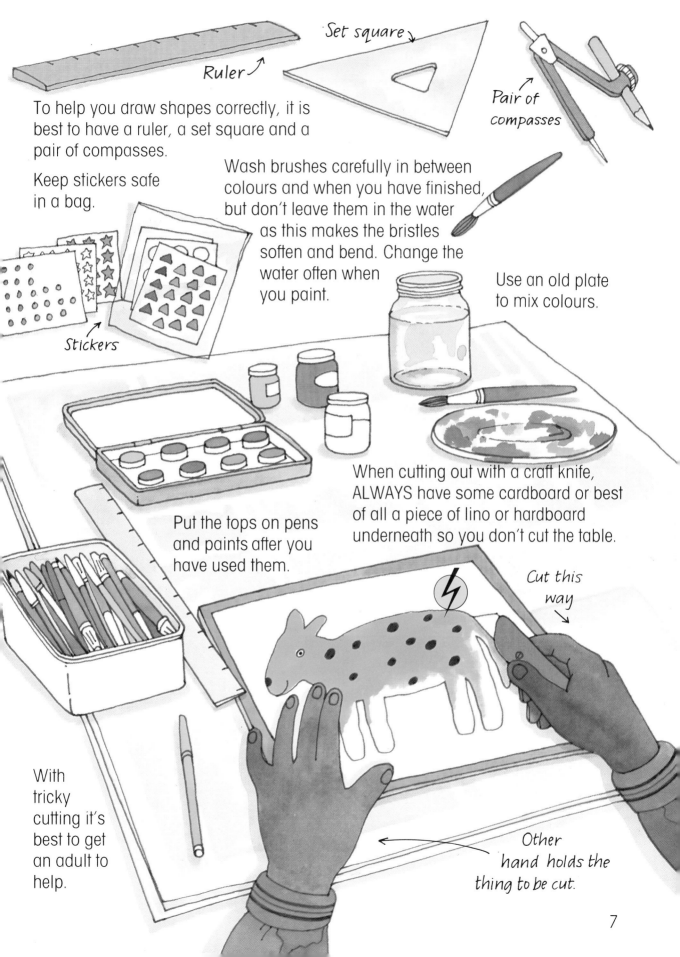

Ruler ↗

Set square ↘

Pair of compasses ↗

To help you draw shapes correctly, it is best to have a ruler, a set square and a pair of compasses.

Keep stickers safe in a bag.

Wash brushes carefully in between colours and when you have finished, but don't leave them in the water as this makes the bristles soften and bend. Change the water often when you paint.

Use an old plate to mix colours.

Stickers ↗

When cutting out with a craft knife, ALWAYS have some cardboard or best of all a piece of lino or hardboard underneath so you don't cut the table.

Put the tops on pens and paints after you have used them.

Cut this way ↘

With tricky cutting it's best to get an adult to help.

Other hand holds the thing to be cut.

Surprise

Thick paper

Cut out a shape like this

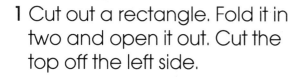

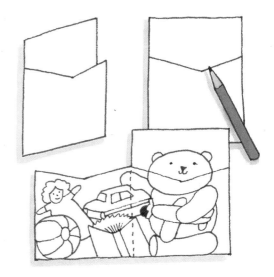

1 Cut out a rectangle. Fold it in two and open it out. Cut the top off the left side.

2 Close the card. Lightly mark the cut edge. Open it and draw a teddy and toys.

Good Luck!

3 Rub out the pencil line and colour in your drawing.

4 Close the card. Draw and colour in the front. Write a greeting here.

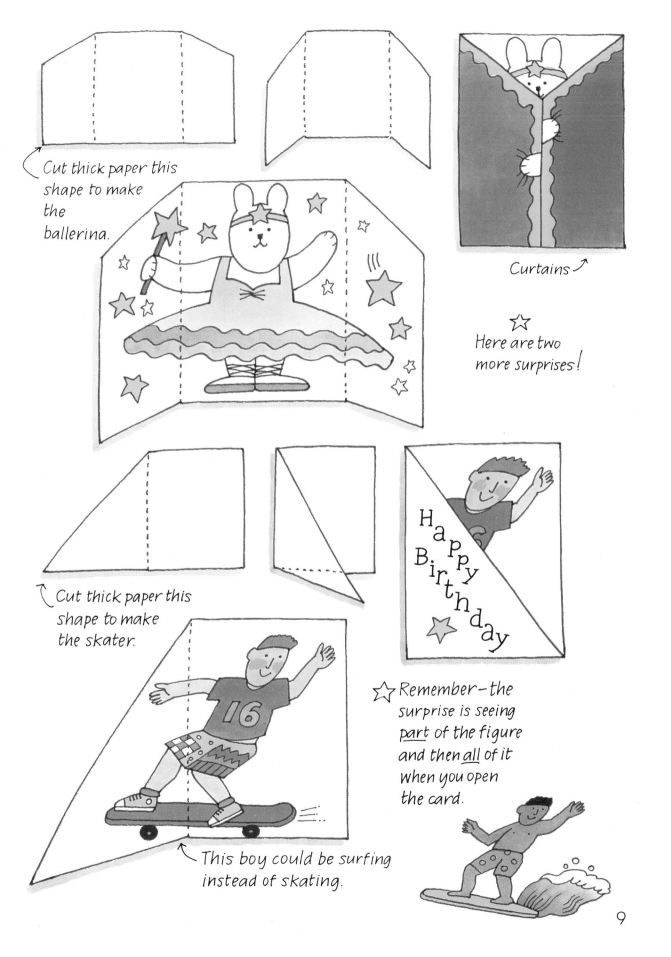

Cut thick paper this shape to make the ballerina.

Curtains ↗

☆ Here are two more surprises!

Cut thick paper this shape to make the skater.

This boy could be surfing instead of skating.

Happy Birthday

☆ Remember – the surprise is seeing <u>part</u> of the figure and then <u>all</u> of it when you open the card.

9

Concertina

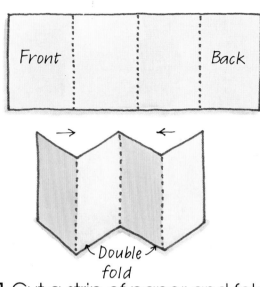

1 Cut a strip of paper and fold it into equal parts.

2 Draw the shape you want. Keep the double fold to the right and cut out shape.

3 Unfold the row of shapes. Decorate them in any way you like. You could use felt-tip pens or stick on pieces of coloured paper. Leave space for your message.

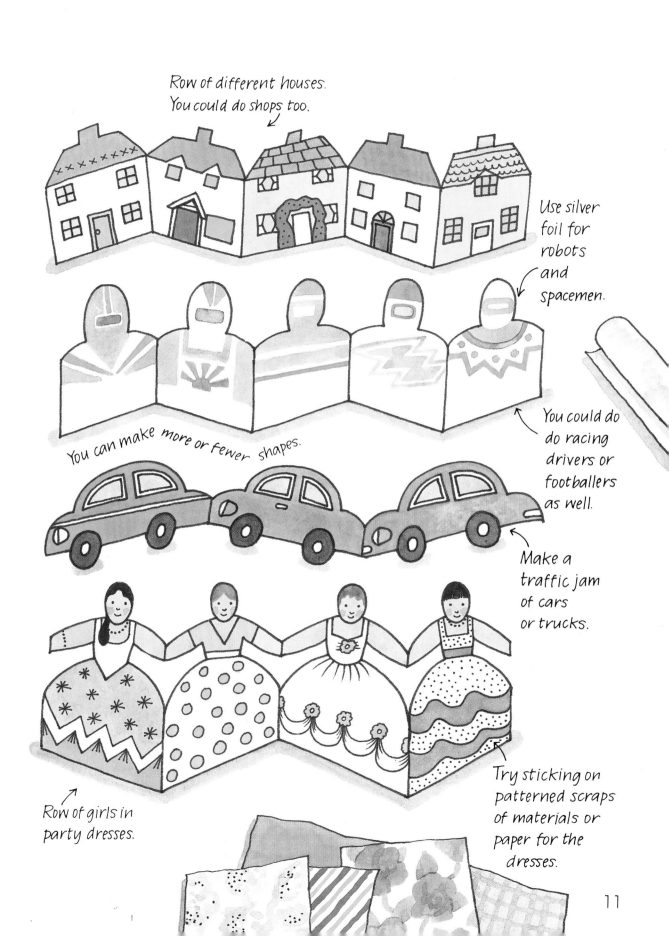

Row of different houses.
You could do shops too.

Use silver foil for robots and spacemen.

You can make more or fewer shapes.

You could do do racing drivers or footballers as well.

Make a traffic jam of cars or trucks.

Row of girls in party dresses.

Try sticking on patterned scraps of materials or paper for the dresses.

11

Secret

1 Cut a rectangle out of thick paper. Fold it in two.

2 Paint or draw a picture of flowers. Use some bright colours.

Message inside bee

3 Draw a bee on a folded piece of paper. Cut it out and colour the top only.

4 Write your secret message inside the bee. Close it and stick it on to the picture.

Message inside gift tag.

Make some secret message gift tags. Thread some wool through a hole made with a paper punch.

Wool

Message inside bird wings.

Row of Christmas cards, one with a message.

Stick on window or door messages.

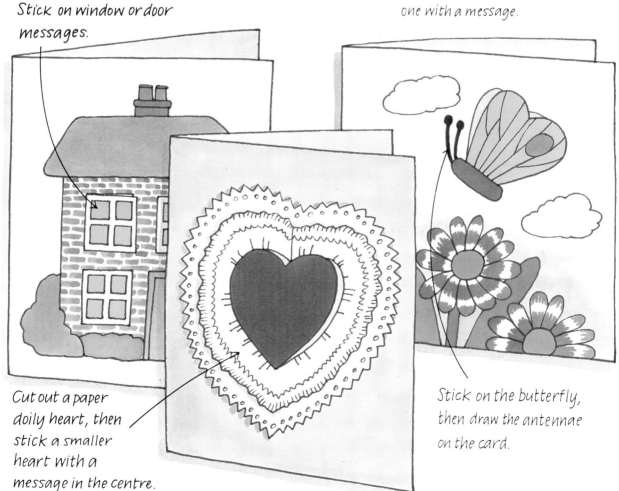

Cut out a paper doily heart, then stick a smaller heart with a message in the centre.

Stick on the butterfly, then draw the antennae on the card.

Zig-zag

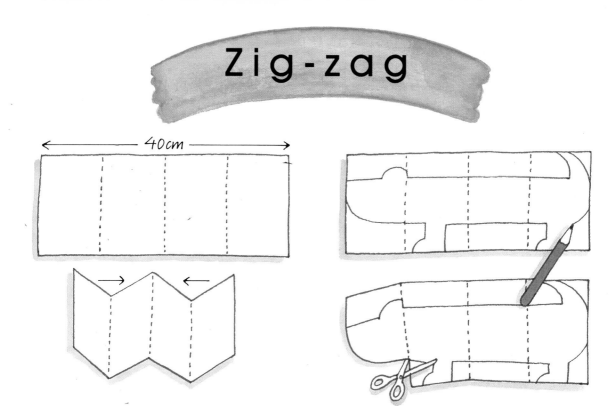

1 Cut a strip of paper and fold it in to four equal parts.

2 Open it up and draw a simple shape like this dog. Cut the shape out.

Enjoy your long holiday!

You could use stickers for decoration.

3 Colour in the shape. The dog could have a bright pattern or a coat. Write a message along him in coloured letters or write on the back of the card.

Katie caterpillar is fun to make.

Draw your family and friends on the train.

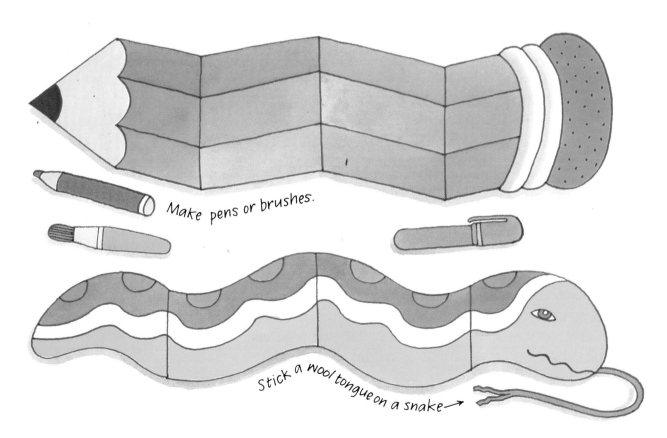

Make pens or brushes.

Stick a wool tongue on a snake →

Stand up

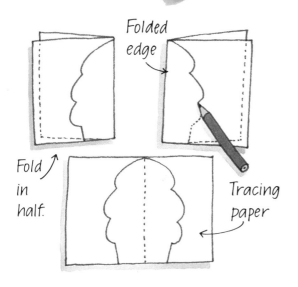

Folded edge

Fold in half.

Tracing paper

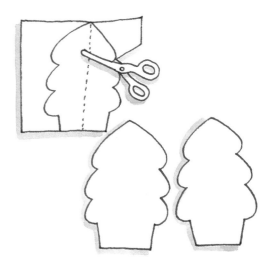

1 Draw half a tree. Turn it over and trace the other half. Open up the paper.

2 Trace the tree on to thick paper. Make two trees and cut them out.

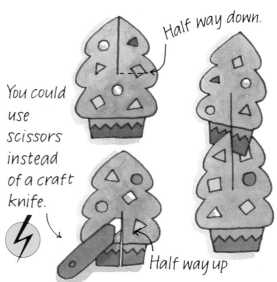

Half way down.

You could use scissors instead of a craft knife.

Half way up

3 Paint or colour all four sides. Decorate them all the same or all different.

4 Lastly, cut two slits – one from the top, one from the bottom. Slot the pieces together.

Try other stand up shapes such as bowls of flowers, people and animals.

GOOD LUCK

Write your message here.

You could decorate your tree cards with flowers, fruit, birds and insects.

17

Pop up

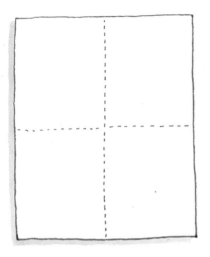

Draw round the edge of a cup or bowl to help you.

1 Cut a rectangle of thick paper and fold it into four.

2 Open it out and draw an arc. Cut along the line with a craft knife.

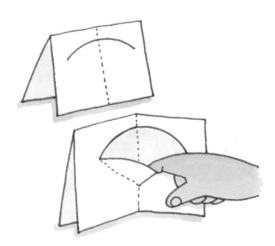

Draw other details too.

Pull the 'pop up' forward to close the card.

3 Fold it into two and then four. Pull out the arc. Close it and press together.

4 Open the card. Draw a person with the face in the 'pop up' and pull it to close.

Here are some ideas for other pop up cards to try. See if you can think of some more.

Get Well Soon!

Write your message inside or on the front of the card.

GOOD LUCK

Draw or stick patterns on the front of the cards.

19

Window

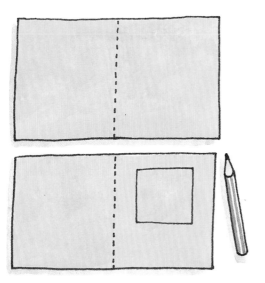

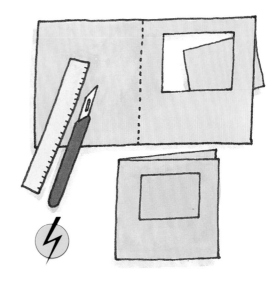

1 Cut and fold a rectangle of card or paper. Draw a window on the right.

2 Cut the window out with a ruler and craft knife.

3 Draw or paint a picture inside. Check you can see it when the card is closed.

4 You could cut out a picture or photograph instead to stick inside.

Use coloured papers.

Decorate around window with stars.

Glue around window and sprinkle glitter.

Write your message here.

Stick patterned paper on the front, cut around the window.

Happy Birthday

21

More ideas

Template cards

Template

Use templates to make lots of similar cards.

Glue on to card.

Add glitter

Cut a template out of card. Draw round it on paper as many times as you want. Cut the shapes out and stick them to plain cards.

Collage cards

Collage cards are a quick way to make lots of similar cards, such as party invitations, thank-you cards or Christmas cards.

Felt tip antennae

Paper wings

Add sticky shapes to your cards.

Use patterned sticky tape.

Cut out shapes in patterned wrapping papers too.

Use pinking shears to cut pretty shapes.

Shaped cards
Cut out simple shapes to make cards, party invitations or gift tags.

Stick shapes on to plain or patterned cards.

Add details with a pen.

Make up shapes of your own.

Tear out shapes with your fingers instead of cutting them.

Printing This is a good way to make several cards quickly.

Footprints and hand-prints in bright paint on coloured paper cards.

Paint your hands or feet with washable paint. Put down plenty of newspaper to stand on!

Paint leaves and press them down on to paper.

Potato cuts are easy to make.

Keep the shapes very simple.